DO YOU KNOW WHAT SOUND THE LETTER B MAKES?

Can you make the B sound?

B says Buh. BUH! BUH! BUH!

Come along with us and let's look at words that start with the letter B!

B is for banana.

Buh

Buh

BANANA

These are bananas.

They are yellow and brown.

Can you tell me more?

You can eat them too!

Let's look at the next page,

get ready to explore!

B is for bee.

Buh

Buh

BEE

This is a bee.

They are yellow and fuzzy.

Can you tell me more?

Bee's make honey!

Let's look at the next page,

get ready to explore!

B is for boots.

Buh

Buh

BOOTS

These are rain boots.

They keep your feet dry

when it is raining outside.

Can you tell me more?

We like to jump in puddles on a rainy day!

Let's look at the next page,

get ready to explore!

B is for beach ball.

Buh

Buh

BEACH BALL

This is a beach ball.

It is round and full of air.

Can you tell me more?

It can float on water!

Let's look at the next page,

get ready to explore!

B is for blueberries.

Buh

Buh

BLUEBERRIES

These are blueberries.

They can be sweet or sour.

Can you tell me more?

They are juicy too!

Let's look at the next page,

get ready to explore!

B is for bus.

Buh

Buh

BUS

This is a school bus.

It is big and yellow.

Can you tell me more?

This bus takes you to school!

Let's look at the next page,

get ready to explore!

B is for bird.

Buh

Buh

BIRD

This is a bluebird.

It has blue and brown feathers.

Can you tell me more?

Bluebirds like to eat bugs!

Let's look at the next page,

get ready to explore!

B is for bath.

Buh

Buh

BATH

The ducks are in the bath.

The bath water is soapy.

Can you tell me more?

Scrub-a-dub-dub, all clean!

Let's look at the next page,

get ready to explore!

B is for bubbles.

Buh

Buh

BUBBLES

These are bubbles.

They are round and float.

Can you tell me more?

Bubbles are fun to pop!

Let's look at the next page,

get ready to explore!

B is for barn.

Buh

Buh

BARN

This is a barn.

It is big and red.

Can you tell me more?

This is where farmers keep their animals!

Let's look at the next page,

get ready to explore?

B is for butterfly.

Buh

Buh

BUTTERFLY

This is a butterfly.

They have wings and can fly.

Can you tell me more?

Butterflies are insects!

Let's look at the next page,

get ready to explore!

B is for boats.

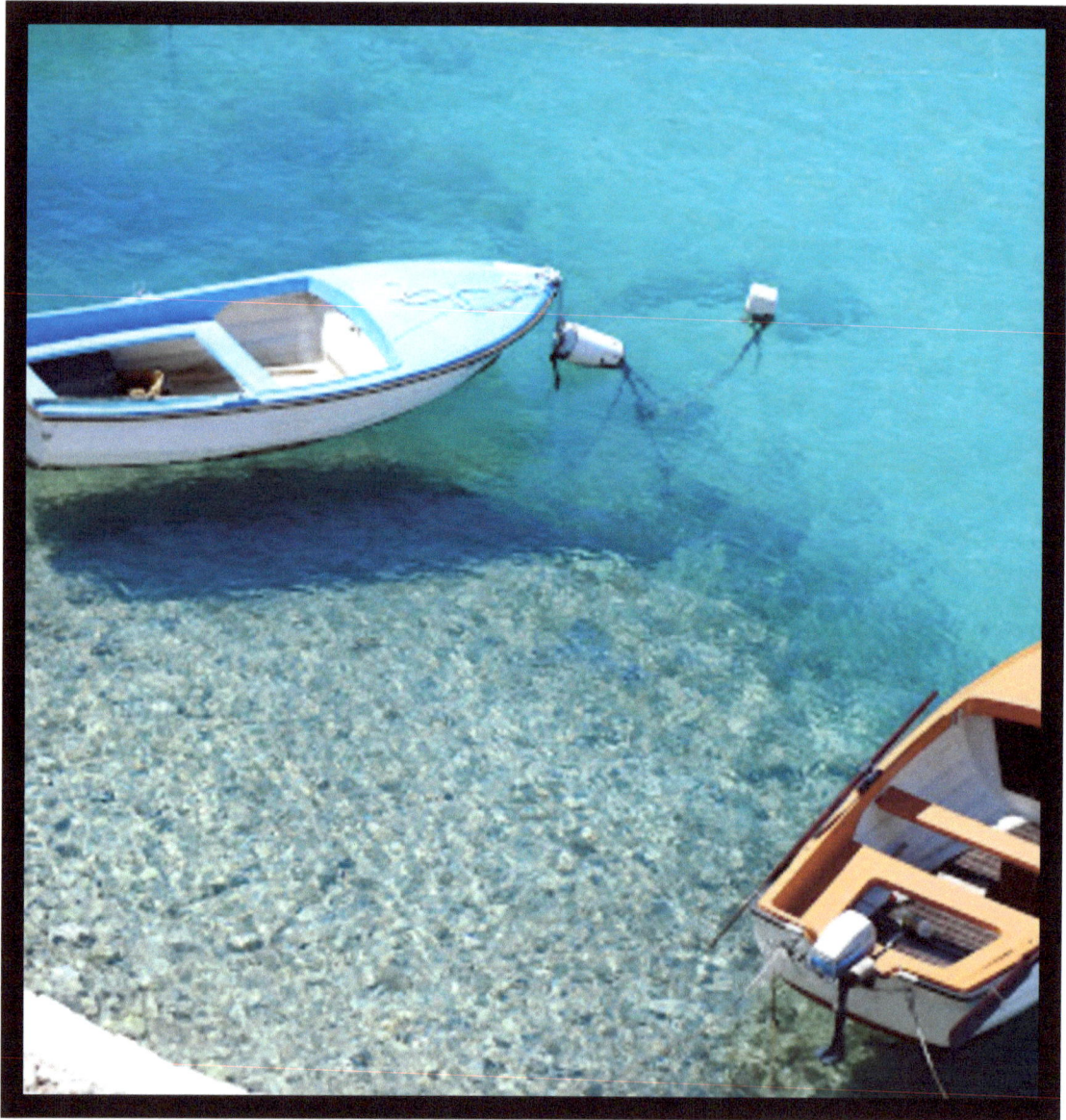

Buh

Buh

BOATS

These are boats.

They are used for travel,

fishing, and fun.

Can you tell me more?

Boats float in water!

Let's look at the next page,

get ready to explore!

B is for bear.

Buh

Buh

BEAR

This is a bear.

The bear is big and brown.

Can you tell me more?

Bears hibernate in winter!

Let's look at the next page,

get ready to explore!

B is for blocks.

Buh

Buh

BLOCKS

These are blocks.

They come in different shapes and sizes.

Can you tell me more?

Blocks are fun to stack and build!

Let's look at the next page,

get ready to explore!

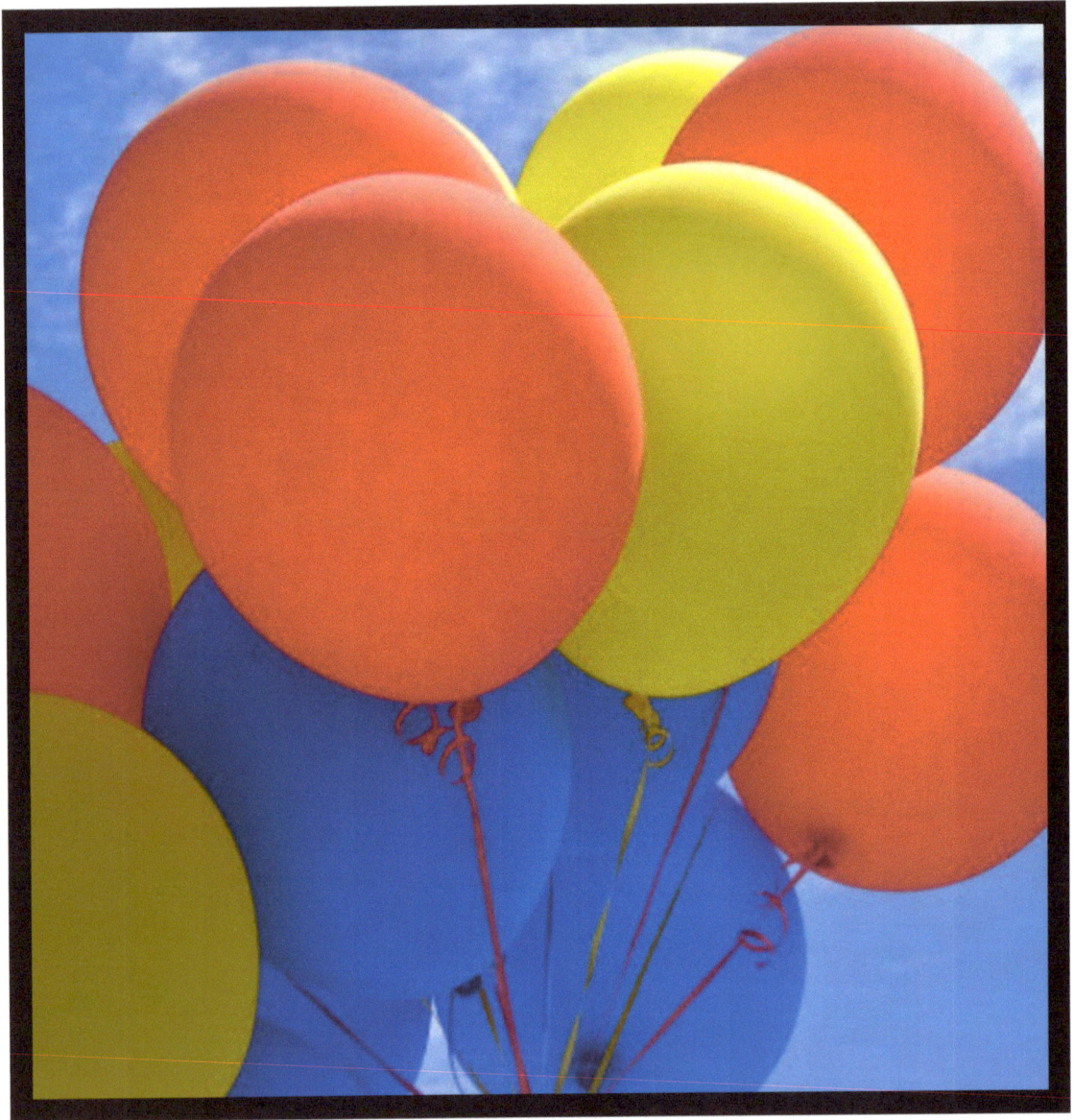

B is for balloons.

Buh

Buh

BALLOONS

These are balloons.

They come in many different colors.

Can you tell me more?

Balloons are filled with helium

gas to make them float!

Let's look at the next page,

get ready to explore!

B is for **b**irthday.

Buh

Buh

BIRTHDAY

HAPPY BIRTHDAY!
Do you know the birthday song?
Can you sing it with me?

🎶 Happy Birthday to you!
Happy Birthday to you!
Happy Birthday dear reader!!
Happy Birthday to you! 🎶

"BIRTHDAY BABY GETS BIG BALLOONS."

CAN YOU SAY IT AGAIN BUT FASTER THIS TIME?

"BIRTHDAY BABY GETS BIG BALLOONS."

COUNT HOW MANY B'S ARE ON THIS PAGE. ____

Tongue Twister answer (12)

THANK YOU
FOR
HAVING FUN
WITH US
AND OUR
LITTLE LESSON
SESSION!

For Lala, Enzo, Deklin, and, Kieran our inspiration.

About Us

Hi there! We're so glad you found us!

We're Towanda and Jem, lifelong friends who have stayed close through the years. Our journey as friends—and now as parents—has led us on a new adventure, inspiring our book creations. Our stories are inspired by our little ones, and we hope to bring joy, learning fun, and inspiration to families with our books. Created with early readers in mind, our stories aim to spark curiosity, imagination, and a love for learning in young minds! Through fun conversations, you can discover what your little ones know and help their knowledge grow with each joyful lesson!

Thank you for reading!
We hope you enjoyed our book.

Be sure to check out the other
titles in our series,
COMING SOON !

Explore More Here !!!

A B C D E F
G H i J K
L M N O P
Q R S T U
V W X Y Z

www.ingramcontent.com/pod-product-compliance
Lightning Source LLC
Chambersburg PA
CBHW041547040426
42447CB00002B/82

9798992674101